SO-BDY-533

Share the Good News

Fr. John Bertolucci

SERVANT PUBLICATIONS
Ann Arbor, Michigan

Available from Servant Publications, Box 8617,
Ann Arbor, Michigan 48107

ISBN 0-89283-260-6
Printed in the United States of America

Share the Good News

WE ARE LIVING in urgent times. The world is in grave peril from many kinds of evils, and the only solution is repentance and salvation. But how are people to repent and experience new life unless Christians introduce them to the Savior, to Jesus Christ?

The process of leading men and women to repentance and conversion to Christ is called evangelism. Every individual who comes to know the Lord Jesus Christ in a personal way is called by him to be an evangelist. This responsibility is even more urgent today given the state of violence and despair that characterizes so much of our world.

There are many different ways to evangelize. Some people are called to stand on street corners and speak about Jesus Christ to all who pass by. Others are called to proclaim the gospel in huge stadiums before television cameras and radio microphones. Others are called to seek out situations where they can present the gospel message to complete strangers, yet in a very natural and personal way. All are called to speak of Christ, of his mercy and his love, to relatives, friends, neighbors, and anyone else the Lord places in our lives.

Christians have used many methods and techniques for leading others to Christ. I will focus on three: 1) intercessory prayer; 2) personal evangelism; and 3) the witness of a holy life.

Prayer Power

Every one of us knows someone we desire to bring to a personal relationship with Jesus Christ. The first and most basic instrument of evangelism is prayer. Prayer is the most powerful weapon we have. Every Christian has at his disposal very great power—the power of intercessory prayer. We must use this power to bring others to the Lord Jesus Christ.

Scripture speaks of prayer as part of the spiritual armaments we put on in order to engage in daily spiritual battle. In the Epistle to the Ephesians, St. Paul describes what the spiritual arms are. At the end of that passage, Paul says: "At every opportunity, pray in the Spirit, using prayers and petitions of every sort . . . pray constantly and attentively" (Eph 6:18).

Many people have told me that they can't pray constantly. But I believe they can. Why do you think God has revived the gift of tongues in this generation? Why do you think the Holy Spirit has been poured out on the Christian people in such abundance? Because the Lord knows that we need to pray at all times and he has given us the tools we need in order to pray constantly.

Every Christian needs a daily prayer time. It is vitally important for us to set aside time each day to worship, to meditate on the word of God, to listen to his voice and to pray in the Spirit. We should have as our goal to set aside at least an hour a day for a formal prayer time. But what about the other twenty-three hours of the day? It is possible, indeed as St. Paul tells us, it is necessary to pray at all times.

How do you do it? Here are a couple of examples: You're driving down the highway on your way to or from work, and you begin praying in the Spirit. Or, perhaps you're listening to someone's complaints about how awful life is. You want them to know the love and peace of Christ, and your tongue moves in quiet prayer for them. Prayer in the Spirit gives you the power you need to pray constantly.

Another way of praying constantly is to speak to Jesus and to the Father in simple ways. This kind of prayer involves simple, direct conversation with the Holy One who lives inside us. We should be able to talk to God at any time, as though he is right next to us, remembering that he is the one who knows and loves us better than anyone else does. This kind of simple prayer, however, is no substitute for formal prayers. We should pray simply and pray in the spirit, but we should also avail ourselves of the liturgy and scriptural prayer. Whenever you are trying to evangelize someone, it's important to realize that prayer is your most important and potent weapon. I have heard many exciting stories about how the power of prayer has been used to "move mountains" in the conversion of people. A few years ago, Father Michael Scanlan and I were flying to an island in the Caribbean. During the flight, we were talking and sharing with one another. After a time, Father Michael began to pray and meditate and I sat there, in the aisle seat, reading from the Liturgy of the Hours. Suddenly, the man sitting across from me looked over and said, "I see you're a Christian."

"Yes," I answered.

"Could you tell me what you're doing?" he said.

I explained that I was praying the Liturgy of the Hours, which is a powerful form of prayer that the Catholic Church has developed from the scriptures and the writings of the men we call the Fathers of the Church.

When I finished my explanation, the man asked if he could share something that had been happening in his life.

"Go right ahead," I replied.

He proceeded to tell me that he had been a communist, that he was in the military of a certain nation, and that he had been trained in Cuba by Soviet agents. One night, while he was on guard duty, he had a sovereign experience of God.

He was at his post, half dozing because it was very late and he was tired. Suddenly, a bright light shone before him and he knew deep in his heart that he was having an experience of One who, according to the communist propaganda, didn't even exist. All of a sudden, he knew he was experiencing God. He felt certain that he could find some kind of explanation about what was happening to him if he could only find a church.

The next day, he did find a church that was open—a rare phenomenon in that particular country. He went in and simply sat there. As he sat in that Catholic Church, he knew he had come home. He was determined to begin living a Christian life, regardless of the consequences.

He told me this and then asked, "Am I all right? Can you tell me anything more?"

I immediately told him how much more of God's love and goodness he could experience by welcoming Jesus Christ into his life and being baptized in the Holy Spirit.

As we talked, he told me that his wife had been praying for him for years. Day after day she had interceded for him. This woman applied the power of prayer to evangelize her husband, even though he was far away in Cuba, being trained by Marxists. I don't know how many years she had been praying, but her perseverance paid great rewards because her husband returned home a man on fire with the love of God.

Each of us should pray faithfully for others to

come to know God, no matter how bleak their lives may seem. As we do this, we will begin to develop a list of people to pray for regularly. We can also ask others to pray for those on our list. For example, you can ask brothers and sisters in your prayer group or church to pray with you for the people on your list during an intercessory prayer time. You don't need to mention the specific names out loud. In fact, it is probably better if you don't. But you can surely say, "Please pray for five friends of mine to come to know the Lord Jesus." A prayer like that will greatly support your own prayer.

I also recommend mentioning the specific names quietly during prayer times at your church worship services. The Catholic liturgy, for example, provides an opportunity for everyone to quietly mention their own intentions during the prayer of the faithful. Catholics should also mention the people they are praying for when they receive communion. Prayers during communion are very powerful. The Lord has his ear inclined to us in a profound way. Take advantage of that! Tell him how much you want to see these people come to know him, to experience his love and grace. He will answer you.

Prayer of Suffering

Once I was preaching at a Christian conference, I looked down in front of me at a section of physically handicapped and elderly people, and the Lord told me to give them a special word.

"I want to make a special point," I told them, "of looking at you my brothers and sisters who are in wheelchairs, or who are otherwise handicapped, and you who are sick or elderly. Some of you may think that you have been put out to pasture, that you are not useful because you can't be as active as younger or healthier people. Don't believe it! You can pray. You can be the powerhouse behind the wave of evangelism that ought to be going on today."

I strongly believe that when people unite their suffering with their prayer, they engage in an especially powerful form of intercession. St. Paul speaks of this very point: "Even now I find my joy in the suffering I endure for you. In my own flesh I fill up what is lacking in the sufferings of Christ, for the sake of his body the church" (Col. 1:24).

I believe that Christians should pray for healing. But I also believe some of the suffering that is attached to sickness, to paralysis, to old age, ought not to be wasted. We can take that suffering, even as we await our healing now, or in the resurrection, and we can offer it for the sake of the church. We can give our suffering to the Lord as a prayer on behalf of his people.

I can't tell you why or how this happens. I just know it's true—God's word says it very explicitly. So when you are sick or suffering in any way, don't think it is unimportant. Don't think it is something to be depressed or angry about. Use your suffering to intercede on behalf of God's people. Such prayers, said patiently day after day for the love of Jesus Christ, can work wonders in the lives of others.

We can see, in the life of the soldier I met on that plane, how effective our prayers can be. No evangelist convinced that young man of the reality of God, no one personally witnessed to him, no one prayed over him. He was sovereignly brought to the Lord by the fervent prayer of someone hundreds of miles away.

Father Scanlan and I see this kind of thing repeated again and again as we travel and on the campus of our college, the Franciscan University of Steubenville. We see many young people, most of whom came to us from situations where there was almost no pastoring, almost no feeding of the word of God, and hardly any youth ministry. Many of these young people were sovereignly evangelized, most likely in response to the prayer of parents or friends, who were patiently praying that the young person would receive the Lord into their lives. Those prayers have been answered.

Pray for Evangelists

We should also pray for those to whom God entrusts the specific ministry of evangelism.

In the passage I quoted earlier from Ephesians 6, St. Paul says, "Pray constantly and attentively." He then goes on to request prayers for his ministry of evangelism: "Pray for me that God may put his word on my lips, that I may courageously make known the mystery of the gospel—that mystery for which I am an ambassador in chains. Pray that I may have courage to proclaim it as I ought." (Eph 6:19-20)

We should all pray that God will bless the evangelists he has raised up. We should pray that he will raise up more lay evangelists. We should pray for those who have been ordained to the official ministry of the church—our pastors and bishops. Pray for them that God would put his word on their lips and that they would courageously make known the full truth of the gospel.

Why should we pray? Because the salvation of many people is at stake. The Bible says, "How shall they call on him in whom they have not believed? And how can they believe unless they have heard of him? And how can they hear unless there is someone to preach?" (Rom 10:14) Pray, then, that God will send the preachers and evangelists necessary to reach our hurting world with the truth of Jesus Christ.

Pray that God will raise up from our midst the evangelists we need. Pray also for the ministers of the gospel he has already raised up, many of whom are discouraged, confused, or otherwise ineffective. Pray for every minister and preacher; and for every priest who stands in any church pulpit in the world. Pray that they will, in the words of Ephesians 6:20, "be able to courageously make known the mystery of the gospel." To proclaim the full gospel as it ought to be proclaimed.

Pray also that God will multiply the fruitfulness of the preaching gifts of those of us he has called to evangelize not only in the pulpit but on radio and television, through books and tapes and magazines, and in classrooms and on street corners.

Another element of supporting those God has entrusted with the ministry of evangelism is to support them with contributions of time and talent, if possible, as well as with financial contributions. Evangelism is a ministry that consumes an enormous amount of personal energy and money. Evangelists need to hear from you. They need your support. And they need an encouraging word now and again.

We need to pray that all the evangelistic gifts of the church will be renewed, revived, and increased. During the 1970s there was a evangelistic flurry of activity in renewal movements, particularly in the charismatic renewal. But as the 1980s dawned, the momentum slowed quite a bit and some people were talking about how the renewal had peaked.

Well, don't you believe it. God is continuing to renew his people. Many who were renewed in the 60s and 70s got bogged down and lost interest. What is needed now, as we move further into the 1980s, is an increase in the number of those who will courageously preach the full gospel of our Lord and Savior Jesus Christ.

The charismatic renewal is one of the most significant revivals of evangelistic activity in the 2,000 year old history of Christianity. During the decades since the Pentecostal movement began in 1901, millions of people have come to know, love, and serve Jesus Christ. Today the Pentecostals are the largest body of Protestant Christians in the world.

When the Pentecostal movement spread to what are called the "mainline" Protestant churches and the Catholic Church, during the 1950s and 1960s, evangelism burst forth in a dramatic way. Millions of church-going people who had become somewhat stale in the Christian life, were re-evangelized and set on fire to spread the message of Jesus Christ throughout their churches. Millions more who had ceased the practice of the faith were attracted by the charismatic evangelists and prayer groups which sprang up just about everywhere.

Today the charismatic renewal continues to attract many thousands of people to a full, personal commitment to Jesus Christ every year. And that is what evangelism is all about.

Evangelism By Sharing

All of us must engage in frequent and fervent prayer that others might come to know the Lord. We should also pray for the evangelists God has called forth and for those he has yet to call. But we must also evangelize others ourselves. We do this best by personal sharing.

This kind of personal evangelism is spoken of in the Epistle of St. Peter: "Venerate the Lord, that is, Christ, in your hearts. Should anyone ask you the reason for this hope of yours, be ever ready to reply, but speak gently and respectfully." (1 Pt 3:15-16)

Everyone of us can and should evangelize in our homes, in the marketplace, in our schools, at work. We share the gospel most effectively when we speak "gently and respectfully" of "this hope of ours," our own vibrant relationship with Jesus Christ, the King of Kings and Lord of Lords.

Do not be mistaken: St. Peter is not just saying that we should wait until someone asks us about our faith. We should also be ready and willing to take the first step whenever appropriate.

The bulk of the work of evangelism in our day is not going to be done by the pulpit preachers, or the TV evangelists, or those who produce Christian books, magazines and tapes. The vast majority of the work of evangelism is going to be done by ordinary men, women, and young people during the course of their daily lives.

Why then, since the Lord has poured out his Spirit so abundantly in our day, is the work of evangelism proceeding so slowly? Why are the majority of people in our families, our home towns, perhaps even our parish, still unevangelized? Because we who have received Jesus and his Spirit are afraid.

We are afraid of what people will say if we start

talking too much about Jesus. We are afraid of being rejected, of being called a fanatic or a holy roller. God forbid that we should fear such rejection. It's a normal part of the Christian life!

The gospel is never spread without cost. Just think of the men and women who have given their lives for the gospel of Christ. Remember Stephen, the first martyr? He suffered an agonizing death because he proclaimed Christ. The martyrs in Rome hung on crosses like the Master himself. Some were soaked in pitch and set on fire as they hung on those crosses. Others went to the lions. Martyrdom has continued throughout the centuries. Every missionary movement has had its martyrs. In our age people are being martyred every day for Christ, especially in the Third World and behind the Iron Curtain. Like their predecessors in ancient days, many Christians today continue to courageously and joyfully proclaim Jesus Christ, even in the face of death.

Certainly you and I can face the comparatively small pain of rejection. Few of us will face bodily suffering if we go out today and share Christ Jesus to friends and neighbors and relatives. We might be rejected, but it is a small price to pay compared to martyrdom. Besides, many times God can use the very rejection we face to bring a person to himself. It has been said that the church was built on the blood of the martyrs. We should be able to say that, in our own families and hometowns, the kingdom of God is being built on the pain of rejection. God can and will use it to bring men and women to a saving knowledge of his Son.

Do you fear being called a fanatic? There are many fanatics in the world today. The powers of hell are fanatics. Marxists are dedicated, committed fanatics for their cause. We who are filled with the Holy Spirit should even be more dedicated because we have a cause worth living and dying for. His name is Jesus Christ!

Once you are no longer afraid to be rejected, even to the point of death, then you will become truly bold. As it says in the word of God: "Who indeed can harm you if you are committed deeply to doing what is right? Even if you should have to suffer for justice' sake, happy will you be. 'Fear not and do not stand in awe of what this people fears.' Venerate the Lord, that is, Christ, in your hearts. Should anyone ask you the reason for this hope of yours, be ever ready to reply, but speak gently and respectfully." (1 Pt 3:13-16)

That passage describes how we should approach evangelism. It describes down-to-earth evangelism, kitchen evangelism, lunch room evangelism, poker party evangelism. This is everyday sharing of the gospel with others who are troubled, hurting, empty, lost, disillusioned, or just bored. These people are everywhere, and they need the hope, the answers to life's problems that come from accepting Jesus Christ in their lives.

Now Peter is saying two things. He is telling

us to be dedicated to Christ, but not to be obnoxious.

This kind of evangelism does not involve playing any games. You don't have to act as though your life is problem-free. You can evangelize others by sharing with them, by saying, "You know, I can identify with the pain you're going through. I have felt the same way. I have gone through the same kind of difficulty. But I want to tell you what I've found. I have found Him who is the source of my strength. I have found the truth that sets me free. I have found that Jesus Christ is alive. I invited him into my life and got to know him in a personal way. Now I can endure the difficulties of life, I can triumph over them because he who won the victory lives in me."

After that, you can tell them your personal story. You can explain what you were going through when someone approached you with the Good News. You can tell them why you grabbed ahold of it and believed it and how your life has changed as a result. Your story may not be dramatic enough for television or for publication, but it will bear fruit, it will attract others to Christ and his saving gospel. And when you stand before God on your own personal judgment day, Jesus will say to you: "As you have confessed me before men, I will confess you before my Father."

Even when it isn't possible to share your testimony, you can sometimes give someone a

Bible or a booklet or a piece of paper with a prayer on it.

One time I was counseling someone who was not yet ready to turn to the Lord. "I know you're not ready right now," I said. "But here is a prayer. When you are ready, just say this prayer, from your heart, every day." This encounter took place in a busy restaurant. I had run out of the prayer cards I usually carry, so I wrote the prayer on the placemat and gave it to the young man. It was a simple prayer and it went something like this:

"Jesus, I am not sure if you're real, but I need you. Come into my life. Have mercy upon me, a sinner. If you are real, show yourself to me and I'll follow you."

Well, that young man kept that placemat, and one day he prayed that prayer, and then he wrote me a letter. "It's happened to me," he wrote. "Jesus is real! I've given my life to him. Hallelujah!"

I've also heard from people years after I first approached them with my testimony. They have told me that someone else continued the work of evangelism that I had begun. Others tell me that they woke up in the middle of the night and experienced the presence of the living God; or that they were worshipping in church and the Lord revealed himself to them.

There are many, many ways to reach people for Christ. Most of these ways are simple and ordinary. They come to us on the spur of the moment when we are ready and willing to be used by God to reach out to someone in his name.

Sometimes, people will immediately respond to the Good News, and you will be able to lead them in a prayer of commitment. Sometimes, you will need to point them in a particular direction. For example, you may need to invite them to attend a prayer meeting or a conference with you.

I know a woman who literally dragged her husband to a charismatic conference. She did it as a last resort. He was an alcoholic and a drug addict, and in the middle of a sermon he was barely listening to—God sovereignly touched him. That man gave his life to the Lord then and there. He was filled with the Holy Spirit and was healed in body, soul, and spirit. Today, he is a strong Christian man. He has resumed his rightful role as husband and father, and he is leading others to Christ.

I know of another woman who makes herself available to God every single day. The Lord brings to her other women who are in need of Jesus. This woman not only shares with them, she brings them to evangelistic luncheons. She not only prays for them, she goes to their homes and prays with them. She not only tells them to read the Bible, she calls them up in the middle of the afternoon and reads to them from the Bible. Many women have come to know their Savior because of this woman's fidelity.

I know of a married couple who conduct a Bible study in their home. They invite neighbors, relatives, and church members to come over and talk about the Bible. After a good discussion and an appetizing snack, they begin talking about Jesus Christ. Many nights someone leaves that home having given their heart and mind and soul to the King of Kings.

None of the people I have mentioned are exceptional. They are ordinary people, but they are dedicated to evangelism because they have experienced the saving power of Jesus Christ in their own lives and because the Holy Spirit impels them to spread the word. They are involved in a kind of evangelism which is happening all over the world because the "little people" of God, the ones who are just ordinary housewives, factory workers, office workers, bank tellers, and students, are beginning to share the gospel. If you are not evangelizing others, you should be! Every Christian is called to evangelize, to win the hearts of men and women to the Lord through prayer and personal witness.

I have told you a number of stories about people who became productive evangelizers. Now I want to tell you how you can also become an effective evangelizer. The first thing you must do is to pray daily for an evangelizer's heart. Ask the Lord to give you the desire, the zeal for souls that other evangelizers have. Ask him to present you with opportunities to evangelize and with the wisdom to go about evangelism in a practical, fruitful way.

None of the people I have talked about became evangelizers overnight. You probably won't either. Each of them had to set some realistic goals, pray every day, and persevere despite the setbacks and the lack of fruitfulness which sometimes occur in evangelism. You will find these things to be true of your evangelism as well.

But do not be discouraged! The Lord our God wants you to be an evangelizer and God is the one living being who always gets what he wants when we cooperate with him. Jesus Christ himself takes an active interest in every case of evangelism. He is the Good Shepherd looking for the lost sheep—you are the vehicle he uses. Don't forget that! And don't get discouraged. Jesus will send his Holy Spirit upon you to give you everything you need: the opportunity, the right kind of attitude, the right words to say. He will also be active in the life of the person you are evangelizing. You will not be alone! Persevere and bear fruit.

I know of a young man named Jim who came to know the Lord Jesus Christ personally in such a dramatic and life-changing way that he dedicated almost every waking minute to evangelizing others. His first several attempts resulted in about every mistake possible. He would preach at people, point out their sins, or initiate a debate on doctrine. He struck out everytime. But he persevered because he knew that the Lord wanted him to be an effective witness.

Instead of giving up, Jim discussed his problem with more mature Christian friends. He also read good books about effective evangelism. And he applied the common sense that he had developed in his own life. The latter was perhaps most beneficial. He found that there was absolutely nothing wrong with applying lessons he had learned on the football field or in math class to his efforts at evangelism.

Jim learned that if people were going to accept his witness, he would have to demonstrate the fruits of the Spirit in his own life. He had to be patient, loving, and kind. He had to be genuinely concerned about the welfare of the people he wanted to evangelize. He had to learn how to speak to them in a way that they could accept. When he learned these simple lessons, he became a very effective evangelizer.

Today Jim is a leader in a large Christian fellowship and is looked to by many people as an authority on evangelism.

Not everyone is called to be an authority on evangelism. But everyone is called to learn how to evangelize effectively. This occurs by applying common sense, the experiences of everyday life, and the teaching of experienced Christian leaders to your own attempts at evangelism.

The Witness of Life

Christians should hunger and thirst for the things God desires. We should pray unceasingly for people who do not know the Lord. We should pray for those who are evangelizing. And we should actively witness whenever we have an opportunity to do so.

Another way in which we let "this hope of ours" clearly show forth is by the witness of our own lives. We belong to Jesus Christ, and we should look and act like we belong to him. Every aspect of our behavior should clearly show that we belong to the Holy One himself. Such behavior will make us stand out among our contemporaries, because most men and women today behave like anything but committed Christians. But we should! We should be leading holy lives. We should be leading prayerful lives. When we do, those who know us will be able to see that we are guided by hope and peace and love. These are the fruits of a holy life, the results of a real, personal relationship with Jesus Christ.

I am not simply talking about standing out because we wear crosses, or have Christian bumper stickers on our cars, or because we carry Bibles around with us. We should stand out because we dress modestly, speak respectfully, and behave righteously. We should stand out because we keep our homes clean and open to hospitality. We should stand out because we are always ready to pray with people, to offer them help with their problems, to support them when they are sick or in need, to laugh and to cry with them.

We certainly do need to have signs of our Christianity around us. We need Bibles; we need Christian art on our walls and Christian music on our stereos; we need to make Christian entertainment our primary form of entertainment; and we should regularly enjoy the fellowship of Christian friends in our homes.

Together with our Christian lifestyle, the fruit of the Spirit will attract some of the people who know us to the Lord. Most Christians have had this kind of experience. One young woman came to know Jesus Christ after leaving home to attend college in another city. She had been a rebellious teenager, getting into trouble at every opportunity. Everyone in her family loved her, but her reputation suffered because of her immature rebelliousness. This young woman had a life-changing encounter with Jesus Christ while at school. The Christians she associated with encouraged her to begin evangelizing others. She decided to start with her own family. But they simply were not prepared to listen to her. Gradually, members of the family began to see that she had indeed changed; that Christianity was more than a passing fad in her life; that she was turning into a polite, kind young woman, they were willing to listen to her witness. They then began to examine their own lives to see what was lacking. The result was that most of the members of that large family came to Jesus Christ, became involved in the charismatic renewal, experienced many dramatic healings, and became evangelizers in their own right, leading dozens of men and women to the Lord.

As was the case with the young woman, our behavior and our character will speak for us saying plainly, "Jesus is the Lord of my life, and I am happy because he is. I am kinder and more polite, more concerned and more careful of others, because Jesus Christ, the one who cares the most, lives in me."

In chapters three and four of the First Letter to the Thessalonians, St. Paul outlines what it means to live as followers of Jesus Christ. I'll only quote one verse of the passage, but I encourage you to read the whole thing and meditate on it: "I exhort you brothers to even greater progress" (see 1 Thes 3:9-4:12).

Don't sit back! God is calling you forward. He wants you to become even holier men and women of God, not by self-righteousness, but by the holiness of the Holy One who has taken over your life—the One who tranforms your body, mind, and spirit by means of daily, ongoing conversion. And when you submit to him, when you grow in holiness, people will notice. They will see you in the daily arena of life, standing in contradiction to the mores of today which lead to bondage, depression, alienation, and death. The fruit of the Spirit leads to happiness, health, freedom, and eternal life. Most people that we know will choose the latter if they see it as a reality in our lives.

The epistles are full of helpful advice about witnessing by the example of your life. "Be prudent in dealing with outsiders; make the most of every opportunity; let your speech be always gracious and in good taste, strive to respond properly to all who address you" (Col 4:5-6). In this passage St. Paul addresses just what I have been talking about: that we witness to others not just with our words, but with our whole life. When we do, they will be attracted by what we have found and ask us about Jesus and why we are living the way we are. This is evangelism, and it can happen normally, day in and day out.

One day, while I was preaching in Vermont, I walked into an ice-cream parlour, full of young people. The whole rock music subculture greeted me. The girl who served me looked at my Roman collar, and I could tell by her glance that she despised what I stood for. Yet, I could also tell that she was unhappy. I just kept smiling at her and loving her as I asked for a rum-raisin cone. Actually, I didn't know if I would even like rum-raisin. I asked for it because she suggested it. My intention was to send out a signal of friendship.

The young lady and I continued to talk while she packed some ice cream for me to take back to the place I was staying. I took advantage of the opportunity to explain something about my Christian philosophy of life. I packed quite a bit into those few minutes, just as she packed as much ice cream as she could into the container.

I don't know when or if she will ever come to the Lord, but I tried to plant a seed, just by being kind, by speaking out, and by showing her some respect while I spoke the word of love. This is the kind of thing St. Paul talks about. Be kind, be respectful, and take every opportunity to speak about Christ and Christian values.

Recently I heard the story of an alcoholic priest. He was known in his diocese as an alcoholic. In fact, some cruel jokes were sometimes told about him. One time this priest attended a service conducted by another priest and was healed of his alcoholism. Because the healing was so complete and so obvious to many people, he was sought out by others who had a problem with alcohol abuse.

The priest's technique was always the same. He counseled those who came to him, telling them first of all that it was impossible for them to deal with their problem on their own. Then he introduced them to the One who could help them—Jesus Christ. Helping people develop a personal relationship with the Lord was the key to his ministry. After that, it was easy to pray for deliverance from alcohol—God always answered those prayers because he was already at the center of the lives of the persons being prayed with.

This priest's ministry was fruitful because people were able to see the change in his own life. His entire life spoke of the power of Jesus Christ. He was a living example of the "before and after" pictures we often see in advertisements for weight-reduction products. People could see how God had worked in his life, and they were willing to trust God to work in their lives too.

We are all called to exhibit that kind of fruit. Don't be put off by people who counsel you "not to wear your religion on your shirtsleeve." You'd better look like a Christian and act like a Christian and speak like a Christian. I don't mean that you should be obnoxious. Quite the contrary. You should be truly Christian—polite, patient, caring. But your Christianity had better show!

Evangelism Is Vital

Evangelism is important because of what is written in the word of God, in Acts 4:11-12. I pray that you will engrave this word on your heart, that you will memorize it and repeat it to yourself day after day. It provides the reason why we must go and win the world for Christ.

This Jesus is "the stone rejected by you the builders which has become the cornerstone." There is no salvation in anyone else, for there

is no other name in the whole world given to
men by which we are to be saved.

(Acts 4:11-12)

The unique and absolute claims of Jesus
Christ are not to be watered down. We are called
to be evangelists, burning with zeal for the
spread of the gospel. In the passage from
Ephesians, chapter six, St. Paul calls zeal the
"footgear" in the armor the Christian is to wear
into daily battle for Christ. We should put on
that footgear every day. We should burn with
zeal for Christ. We should hunger and thirst for
his holiness and for his kingdom. An important
aspect of that hunger and thirst is zeal for souls.
It must be an important part of our daily lives.

As I have said, prayer is the greatest weapon
we have to accomplish this. God will answer our
fervent, zealous prayers, and he will raise up
preachers and evangelists, both clergy and lay.
All of us will support the work of evangelists by
attracting people to the Christian way of life as
we share our faith and as we live lives of holiness.

Every Christian is also called to cooperate
with what God is doing in the building up of
support systems for spiritual growth. Today
there are prayer groups, Bible studies, parish
renewal programs, and many other means that
the church is using to provide people with
spiritual nourishment. We who have been renewed in the Holy Spirit need to be involved in

those groups. We need to be able to bring people to Jesus and to point them in the direction of a support system that will continue to nourish and feed them.

The responsibilities of evangelism, when added to everything else that men and women are doing these days, means a very busy daily life. But don't get discouraged! I have discovered that when you really become wholehearted for Jesus and the full gospel, a lot of very good things happen. Three stand out:

1. You will become fearless and courageous in standing up for the gospel and leading others to Christ.

2. You will have an inner joy that no one can take from you.

3. You will be called to lay down your life again and again through inconvenience, pain, suffering, and perhaps even death. But as you do, other people will be saved.

"No test has been sent you that does not come to all men," St. Paul writes in the First Letter to the Corinthians. "Besides, God keeps his promise. He will not let you be tested beyond your strength. Along with the test, he will give you a way out of it so that you will be able to endure it." (1 Cor 10:13)

God may permit us to suffer and struggle, but he will come to our aid. We will triumph because he has triumphed, and we belong to him. Christians today have to believe together, pray together, work together, and struggle together for the sake of the gospel. We have to believe in the full gospel message. We have to live it and proclaim it, with our entire lives.

We must never forget the people we know who are lost in disbelief and sin. We must never forget about the secularism in the church and in our western society. We must never forget the threat of atheistic communism, which is creeping up on believers on every continent. We must never forget the growing force of militant Islam, which is choking out Christian faith in many places.

There is so much work that God has for his people today. And the primary work is leading men and women to Christ Jesus and helping them find sustenance and spiritual growth.

Pray today that the fire of God's Spirit will come upon you. That he will give you the grace you need to grow in your own life and in your local church. That he will plant a flame in your heart so that you will burn with a zeal to want to bring at least one other person to Jesus Christ before you die.

What an opportunity you have to stand before the Lord on your own judgment day and know that you were in some way responsible for at least one person entering heaven with you.

Take that as a minimum goal. I hope you bring many more. But make it your commitment to Jesus to bring at least one other person to him.

All praise be to Jesus, the Advocate, the Alpha and Omega, the First and the Last, the Great

Amen. Blessing and glory be to him who is the Apostle of Our Profession, the Author and Finisher of Our Faith, the Captain of Our Salvation, the Chief Cornerstone, Emmanuel, Everlasting Father, Faithful Witness, Head of the Church, Horn of Salvation, the I Am, the Messiah, the Morning Star, the Power of the Kings of the Earth, the Savior, the Shepherd and Bishop of Souls, the Son of the Most Blessed, the Son of Righteousness, the Wonderful Counselor, Mighty God, Word of God, the Sword of the Spirit, Word of Life, Lord of Lords, and King of Kings.

Father John Bertolucci, a priest of the diocese of Albany, is a well-known evangelist. He appears on the weekly television and radio program "The Glory of God" and is assistant professor of theology at the Franciscan University of Steubenville. He is author of *On Fire with the Spirit.*